PRAISE FOR *10 PRINCIPLES OF THE LIFE OR DEATH OF A SALESPERSON*

In reading Virgil's book, you feel like you are discovering the long missing pieces of the sales puzzle. There are plenty of "how to" sales books, but this book lets readers discover the " Why": Why do your core values make you successful in sales? Why does analyzing your journey make all the difference? Why does integrity and clarity matter? This book builds a life structure in which the main pillars speak to sales. Talk is cheap, but the essence of sales comes from the soul.

Jeff Thatcher, Founder
Discrete Wireless & Wherible GPS Products

Every young person who is starting a sales career needs to read this book as a mandatory action item. This is the path down the road of knowledge that many will discovery on their own one day. The question is how long will it take? How many times will they go on probation for poor sales performance? How many sales opportunities will they blow because they didn't allow the customer to feel their requirements were the motivating factor driving the sale, not the seller's personal gain? Virgil eloquently lays it out in this book.

Glenn Barnes, High-Volume Sales Specialist
Xerox Corporation (30 years)

In 10 Principles of the Life or Death of a Salesperson, Virgil has identified the fundamental principles which separate the good from the great. This book teaches techniques that lead to success for those who implement them.

John Robinson, Pharmaceutical Sales Manager

10

PRINCIPLES

OF THE LIFE OR DEATH OF A
SALESPERSON

VIRGIL BLOCKER

CONTENTS

INTRODUCTION

In an age when a person is a brand and their social media output is a commodity, the salesperson who wishes to have a successful, sustainable career must be able to do more than make cold calls and create a solid sales pitch. Today, potential customers want to buy into the salesperson before they purchase the goods or services being sold. The savvy salesperson invests as much or more into developing personal principles their customers will connect with as they do in cultivating their sales strategy.

When I first met with Virgil to assist him with bringing this book to fruition, I didn't think of myself as much of a salesperson. I considered myself to be a writer and aspiring writing coach whose passion was to help others share their story. Despite being able to check off all the must haves for people selling goods or services online—a website, social media presence, and email list—I wasn't booking the clients or selling the number of books I wanted. Through my interactions with Virgil, I began to understand the reason I wasn't making sales had more to do with my whether I adhered to the principles he espouses in the pages of this book.

Each moment of Virgil's twenty-plus years of sales experience has been carefully considered and mined to produce the masterclass on success in sales you hold in your hands. Each principle is one he has put into practice in a career boasting fifteen President's Club Awards and numerous other industry accolades. These are not trendy techniques that will be useless when times change, but proven principles you can continue to utilize and profit from for the rest of your career.

10 Principles of the Life or Death of a Salesperson isn't just another sales book promising to make you a better salesman if you adopt a certain trendy sales technique; this book promises to change *you,* the person behind the sales pitch. It's no secret that people want to do business with individuals who understand what they need and will work diligently to ensure they get it. They want someone who is organized and exhibits a level of integrity in what they do. In short, they want someone they can trust.

I'm still learning and growing in my journey to be a better salesperson, but the one thing I've realized is most people need to be sold on you and your ability to see and meet their needs before you can sell them anything else. In the following pages, you will be taught ten of the most important characteristics you need to be a better salesperson. Moreover, learning and implementing each one will ultimately make you a better person. When this happens, your products and services will sell themselves.

Erica D. Hearns
Serious Season Publishing

CHAPTER ONE

TRUST

WHAT IS TRUST?

Trust is defined by Webster's Dictionary as, "quite often the attitude that we display towards people who we believe and to a degree hope will be trustworthy." Trust and trustworthiness are similar, yet different. In a perfect world, those we trust will be trustworthy, and those who are trustworthy will be trusted.

Trust is often mistakenly overlooked and taken for granted. Often, sales professionals are completely unaware of its value. It's important when working with your coworkers and customers because it allows you to form and develop effective relationships for support, advice, and/or approval. Since trust often involves associated risk, it can often be perceived as very dangerous. Trusting another person with your personal thoughts or professional ideas invites the risk of betrayal.

In order for trust to be validated in any relationship, both parties involved must express their willingness to trust each other. There are other conditions for trust and trustworthiness, but you should keep this at the forefront of your thoughts as you work with your peers and customers. By doing this, you are able to concentrate on effective listening and your choice of words in your discussions. The question I often ask myself is, "Do my words and actions support the direction I foresee our relationship taking?"

When working with coworkers and customers, I make every attempt not to disagree with their positions in discussions. It's not my goal to show them that I can support my positions in life. I simply listen for understanding while giving nonverbal gestures like head nods to show my understanding. I often use words like, "good point," "that's a great idea," or "I understand." My goal in building trust is to remain in a position of listening, understanding, and support until the time is appropriate for me to clearly express my thoughts, ideas, or concerns.

> *When I was in high school, I had a friend named David. David was a very nice guy who seemed to get along with everyone. It often amazed me how people simply enjoyed his company with such ease. Being the thinker I am, I asked myself the question, "What makes people seem to really like David once they meet him?"*
>
> *After almost 10 years of pondering this question and wondering what magical power David had that I was missing, I asked myself what it was about our relationship I enjoyed. I realized the one thing that stood out about David was that he would take the time to hear whatever thoughts someone had about any topic or concern in life, and never made a personal judgment about the person or where his or her thoughts or ideas came from. Instead, he would simply support the person's thoughts and ideas. This was the key component that separated him from*

other friends. This was what made him different and likable.

Studying David, a principle became clear to me: people don't care how much you know, but how much you care and support them. This supportive approach continues to serve me well when working with coworkers and customers. It allows me to better understand them, support their visions, and build their trust at the same time.

You're probably asking yourself, "Is this possible?" How can you control your tongue instead of expressing your opinions? What I always keep at the forefront of my mind is that it's not about me. It's about being in position to build trust and better understand the customer's thoughts, feelings, and business requirements.

WHAT IS THE POTENTIAL FOR THE BETRAYAL OF YOUR TRUST?

Potential for betrayal can be another condition of trust. As noted above, the corresponding condition for trustworthiness is the power of betrayal. Annette Baier writes that, "trusting can be betrayed or at least let down, and not just disappointed" (1986). In her view, disappointment is the appropriate response when one relies on someone to do something but does not trust him or her to do it. People who monitor and constrain other people's behavior and do not allow them to prove their trustworthiness may rely on others, but they do not trust them. Their reliance can be disappointed, but it can't be betrayed. You can rely on inanimate objects such as alarm clocks, but when they break, you aren't betrayed, although you may feel disappointed. Reliance without the possibility of betrayal is not trust. Thus, people who rely on one another in a way that makes betrayal impossible do not trust one another.

One condition for trust is that the truster accepts some level of risk or vulnerability (Becker 1996). Minimally, what the truster risks, or is vulnerable to, is failure by the trustee to do what the truster depends on that person to do. The truster might try to reduce this risk by monitoring or imposing certain constraints on the behavior of the trustee; but after a certain threshold, the more monitoring and constraining s/he does, the less s/he trusts that person. Trust is relevant, "before one can monitor the actions of ...others," (Dasgupta 1988, p. 51) or when out of respect for others, one refuses to monitor their actions. Therefore, a refusal to be vulnerable tends to undermine trust or prevent it from occurring at all.

HOW DO YOU ESTABLISH A FOUNDATION OF TRUST?

Let me give you example of what I have done on every sales job I've had since my first Marketing Representative sales position. After the first few days on the job or during office orientation, I identify my administrative support staff and my assigned service support manager. Lastly, I identify the team of service technicians who are responsible for maintaining equipment or products within my territory.

These are key components for several reasons. First, when you take the time to meet with your administrative support, this gesture shows a form of honor and respect. This allows you to gain a better understanding of the personality of the administrative support person or group of persons you are working with. I often take notice of items or pictures on their desks and walls. You will find that in an office environment, people are still human and make choices. What people choose to have in the confines of their personal space represents who they are and what they value. Often the items are personal and represent endearment or sentimental value. Each of these items has a story behind it that is near and dear to the person. I never take these items for granted. This gives me a chance to inquire so I may have a better understanding of the life inside the person.

Effective listening is also a huge component in building a foundation for trust. When I first meet with coworkers, listening plays a key role for me. After I observe with admiration and inquire positively about the personal items, I ask the administrative support staff to share with me the company's process for order submission, reports, timesheets, expense reports, etc. This is a vital part in understanding the office protocol, and it also helps to begin to build trust. What I am attempting to establish is trust through showing respect for the administrative support position, my willingness to hear the process, and understand and implement information. This allows me to practice best practices and build my relationship with the administrative support team.

How I have chosen to work with support staff such as Service Managers is very similar. As a Marketing Representative for Xerox Corporation and Eastman Kodak, immediately after coming back from training, I was eager and ready to contact the local Service Managers who were responsible for handling my assigned territory. I made it my business to sit down with the manager and attempt to understand what they expected from me as the Marketing Representative. It's important to understand what they felt was the best way to communicate with their service staff when I had issues or concerns, and to attempt to understand who on their assigned team was responsible for working on and servicing equipment within my assigned sales territory. I would also find out if there was a service lead program that would reward the service representatives if they would turn in leads. To my surprise, quite often there was. This was something I could use to communicate my sales cycles in advance with my service technicians so they would know to turn in leads and be in position once I closed the deal to get credited and rewarded for the sale.

Rewarding the people who support accounts in my territory is a big deal for me. My goal always was and still is to build trust through support. I believe very strongly that a sales professional must be willing to serve the support staff around him to build a good foundation for trust. These are the people behind the scenes who make you great. No one person is an island, but some people believe they can do everything themselves. The real reason those people stay isolated is because of their own greed and desires.

After identifying my service teams, I organized monthly breakfast or lunch meetings and paid for them at my own expense. This yielded great returns. I would start every meeting off by asking the team how I could make their jobs easier regarding machines in the field that may be causing problems, or customers who may be relaying issues. Quite often, they would share with me the aging machines that needed to be updated and were causing them multiple service calls per month. Sometimes they would complain the machines were not located in acceptable areas for them to be serviced. I loved when I received these concerns. Every concern was an opportunity for me to make contact with the customer, but not before I went back to the office and did my homework on the customer. I reviewed the customer account with the service technician, pulled the service logs, and worked up an upgrade plan for new machines or additional equipment.

The upgrade plan for the proposed new product must not be taken lightly. My feeling has always been that when your preparation meets an opportunity, you are in the best position to make the sale. As I spoke with the service technicians, I would often ask them if they had a good relationship with the customer. When they would tell me yes, I would simply ask them if it was ok for me to call the customer, and could they travel with me to our next meeting. Remember, this is a matter of quickly establishing credibility through the already established trusting relationship the service technician has with the customer.

Let me give you an example of one of my largest deals as an Account Manager with Eastman Kodak. I wanted to give a proposal to upgrade all eighteen of this company's Kodak imaging machines, but I could not get the main contact to return my calls to make the appointment. I shared what I was trying to propose to this customer with my service technician at our monthly service meeting. My service technician told me I should let her get in touch with the customer for me. Within two business days, the customer called me and said, "I don't talk to sales people.

However, since your service tech that I've known for seven years came in my office today and shared with me all of the reasons why I should consider upgrading to the new machines, I want you to come in and let's see about upgrading." That deal was a $350,000 transaction, which was all completely initiated by the trust between the service tech and the customer. This was a clear sign my thoughts and ideas about the value of trust were important and correct. As a result, I was able to make sure the service technician placed the lead in and got rewarded for her lead, and I was able to make the sale.

HOW DO YOU BEGIN TO TRUST?

Consider my view that trust can't be willed on a person, but rather is developed over time, Baier questions whether people are able to trust simply because of encouragement to trust (1986, 244). She writes, "'Trust me!' Is for most of us an invitation which we cannot accept at will- either we do already trust the one who says it, in which case it serves at best as a reassurance, or it is properly responded to with, 'Why should and how can I, until I have cause to?'" Baier believes we cannot trust for purely motivational reasons or just because we want to; instead, we must have reason to think the other person is trustworthy.

Becoming an expert professional salesperson, you must take the time to evaluate yourself in the following areas of trust. Connect with specific areas identifying why you may be having problems trusting your coworkers and/or why your coworkers have difficulty trusting you. When you get in front of your customers, they are likely to be able to discern the same concerns others see and experience with you.

BELIEFS OF NON-TRUSTING INDIVIDUALS

1. People are out to get all they can from me, so I must avoid trusting in order to survive.
2. No person should be trusted.
3. Everybody here is out to get me.
4. No one respects me.
5. Never let your guard down or chaos will follow.
6. I will never express my true feelings again. If I do, someone will use them against me to hurt me.

STEPS TO BUILDING A TRUSTING RELATIONSHIP

1. **Be willing to be patient**. Patience does not demand to have its own way. Consider the opinion of others and take their thoughts into sincere consideration. Your patience will often allow you to see more options. The lack of patience will take options away.

2. **In all accounts, demonstrate respect.** Respect is an attitude of acknowledging the feelings and interests of another party in a relationship, and of treating as consequential for the self the helping or harming of the other. Respect does not necessarily imply deference, but a respectful attitude rules out unconsidered selfish behavior. In the words of Malcolm S. Forbes, "You can easily judge the character of a man by how he treats those who do nothing for him." What are your actions

communicating about you?

3. **Eliminate the blame game.** Finger pointing, assigning fault, or condemning others' mistakes diminishes trust. This ferret-out approach instills fear instead of innovation, reduces engagement instead of errors; and reinforces scapegoating instead of accountability. But people who step up to accept their mishaps and acknowledge their mistakes build trust, enhance accountability, and enable future-focused solutions.

4. **Cultivate self-awareness.** Do you stop to consider how your actions, including your words, affect others, or do you operate in a sea of self-absorbed cluelessness? Your answer is tied to your current trust building capacity. Those who operate with thoughtful self-reflection enable trust building; those who don't erect trust barriers.

5. **Do not dishonor others in words or deed.** If your intentions are honorable, your actions are more likely to be perceived by others as trust-building. If you're out to deceive or manipulate, to "win" no matter the approach, the resulting behavior typically broadcasts no-trust. Most of us don't operate with deliberate dark-side intentions, but instead find work challenges in varying shades of gray. Operating from integrity and positive intention offers a path toward trust no matter how gray those situations may appear.

6. **Don't be Selfish.** Those who operate in this age-of-me with an eye on the greater good, a philosophy of contribution, and an understanding of the inter-

connection and interdependence that builds a better future for everyone create trusting relationships. Those who cling to myopic self-interests don't.

WHY EFFECTIVE LISTENING MATTERS

Listening with a sincere attempt to understand is the first step in building a trusting relationship with your coworkers and customers. Effective listening "requires conscious effort and continued practice" (Thompson, Grandgenett, & Gradgenett,1999, p. 8). "A perceived failure to listen is often interpreted by the speaker as a sign of not caring, whereas the perception that the receiver is listening is viewed by the speaker as a caring behavior" (Bulach, Pickett, & Boothe, 1998). "Listening first helps the listener to understand what is being said and adds value at the beginning of the relationship. Empathetic listening (also called active listening or reflective listening) is a way of listening and responding to another person that improves mutual understanding and trust" (Salem, 2003). "This type of listening is an act of acknowledging and identifying the feelings of a speaker while relaying the facts being stated." The listener can practice this by using statements such as, "You feel _____ when the (described event happens)." Emotionally, attempting to review the speakers' concerns will assist in establishing effective and supportive communication between the listener and the person speaking.

VALIDATE

This gives value to feelings regarding what has been stated. Restating to the listener what was heard to clarify gives the speaker a chance to make their points clear. Restatement of what you have heard makes it clear listening has occurred. Validation when one is listening does not mean you agree or disagree with what has been stated. This simply acknowledges you've heard what was stated. This is an act to neutralize and normalize a feeling.

PROBLEM SOLVE

When attempting to solve a problem, don't place your focus on the problem for the purpose of resolution. You must place your energy in the following six steps of the problem-solving process, according to 1000ventures.com, to find answers.

1. Identify and define the problem.
2. Proceed positively, identify causes, and generate alternative solutions.
3. Evaluate the alternative solutions.
4. Make a clear decision.
5. Implement the decision, assign clear responsibility for carrying out the decisions, and set deadlines for completion and review.
6. Follow up, monitor the implementation, compare actual results with expected outcomes and adjust the course of action accordingly.

IMPLEMENT

Make your choice from among your best possible alternatives! It is important to make a clear choice and define a time limit for an attempt to reach your goal. Do it (implement your decision). Do not worry about being successful. Just do it and see what happens!

EVALUATE

Now it's time to see what happened. If you have been successful... great! You should think about a reward for your efforts!

DO YOU TRUST YOUR DECISIONS?

Do your decisions expose your hidden secrets? This question is one you will encounter at some point in your professional career. You can ponder this in difficult times. After fifteen years in sales as a top performer for several fortune five hundred companies, I have often wondered, "Why should the people I'm asking to trust me do so?" Those we are surrounded by on a daily basis make a conscious or unconscious decision whether to trust us or not.

It is my belief that our daily decisions are heavily based on what we have learned or experiences we've encountered. Sometimes what we've learned, whether right, wrong or indifferent, holds us captive to the past and prevents us from growing and maturing in the future. You will find this thinking difficult and challenging for you as you continue to grow as a person and as a professional.

Each one of us perceives ourselves in one manner, while the outside world may perceive us in a completely different manner. It is my belief that in order to understand yourself and how the world perceives you, to grow in life, you need something you can look at (a mirror) that will show you who you are from the inside to the outside. This mirror must remain constant and unchanging. It must be your pillar of truth, the foundation of what you believe. It must have the ability to show you what is true about yourself.

For me, that mirror is the spiritual teachings of Jesus Christ. This is not about religion. This is truly about finding spiritual principles in life you believe work for you. There must be something you can't manipulate for your convenience. It must create balance and be based on love that doesn't change.

I have observed that all of Jesus' teachings start with the learner having to make a change. All our behaviors are seeds that are sown in our lives. We are simply living in the harvest of the seeds we've planted for our lives. This concept is referred to as seedtime and harvest time. This is often difficult for those who have no desire to change their way of thinking, simply because they believe their way is the only way that's right. However, they know in their hearts their way is not working well for them. The outcomes are sporadic and often unpredictable.

Over the years in business, I have taken the time to hear, understand and do what Jesus taught. I am encouraged and amazed that through years of attempting to become a better person and excel in my personal and professional sales career, not one of His principles has ever failed to yield a harvest based upon the seeds I've planted. I'm able to forecast my outcomes by doing what He taught, by taking His teachings and spiritual principles and implementing them.

For example, Jesus taught "Perfect love will cast out fear." What does this mean in your business and professional life regarding building trust? This means the love you have has stages it will go through when building trust. You will have to make a conscious decision to put forth the effort to perfect love through trust. Love must be perfected in you through the following actions: patience, kindness, long suffering, understanding, not being arrogant, and not being judgmental.

You will need to have boldness on days you're feeling challenged in your actions or decisions you've made to trust another person. Your actions will stand as trustworthy when you demonstrate you've done all that is taught to perfect your trust through deliberate acts of love.

Another spiritual principle I use is, "There is no fear in love, but perfect love casts out fear, because fear torments." We must remember he who fears has not been made perfect in trusting in love (again, being patient, kind, forgiving, understanding, not judgmental, and long suffering). By trusting and practicing these ideas, your love is made perfect in you through trust. In order for this principle to work, one must trust these actions are trustworthy in order to be in a position to receive the possible promised outcome. Remember, people are not concerned about how much you know, but they can identify with how much you care.

This has been a pillar of my foundation to better understand myself and the impact I have on others around me in building trust. This principle is an area I've been challenged to improve on a daily basis. This by no means will be made perfect in you by practicing it one time. One of the reasons I love Jesus' spiritual teachings is because they have a way of piercing your heart from the inside and planting themselves in your mind. Ultimately, if you are willing to implement the teaching, you will change. Others around you will observe this change, then they will change in response. You'll be able to observe a difference in them in turn.

ACTIONS TO PRACTICE

- ✓ Listen to others without expressing your opinion on every topic.
- ✓ Lose your fear of making yourself vulnerable to betrayal.
- ✓ Take time to understand how you can support your team and reward them for supporting you.
- ✓ Follow the five steps to building a trusting relationship.
- ✓ Find an unchanging mirror by which you can reflect upon your decisions and how they are perceived by others.

CHAPTER TWO

RESPONSIBILITY

In the game of golf, every player is responsible for playing his or her own ball. Other people can give you tips, instructions, or coaching. However, at the end of the day, you must swing the club, hit the ball and move it toward the hole, or you don't score. Likewise, in sales, salespeople often have managerial, administrative, and technical support teams. However, it is ultimately the salesperson's responsibility to keep the sales cycle moving forward and eventually close the sale. Along the journey, you may seek and receive advice or counsel from many sources, but at the end of the month, it's your responsibility to achieve the monthly sales quotas.

WHAT IS RESPONSIBILITY?

- Responsibility is taking care of your obligations in an acceptable timeframe.
- Responsibility is maintaining accountability for your actions.
- Responsibility is always preserving your trustworthiness.

Your views on responsibility are vital to the foundation of your career in the field of sales. Employers often assume someone hired to perform a sales job have a sense of responsibility. I've worked in sales for over twenty years. I've sat in on many interviews as a sales manager. I've never heard an employer ask a single question pertaining to a prospective employee's views on responsibility.

You can use the following list to help identify who and what you care about and are responsible for.

1. Are you married or single?
2. If you are married, does your spouse work?
3. Do you have children?
4. Are you responsible for taking care of anyone else?
5. Are you responsible for any employees?
6. What are your financial obligations?

Identifying who or what your actions directly affect in advance can be a monumental source of strength and motivation in unpredictable, difficult times. I have always found it's better not to wait until conditions become troubling to use your responsibilities as a source of motivation. Identifying who and what you're responsible for proactively becomes a source of fuel to the flame of your desire to meet and/or exceed your goals. You will work with more focus and intensity if your motivation comes from someone or something you care deeply about than if you're competing with someone else or meeting a sales quota posted on a wall.

How can understanding who and what you are responsible for be a source of motivation? In the field of sales, you will have times when you can't reach your goals, times when you come close to reaching your goals, and times when you barely exceed your goal or quota. Keeping who or what you care most about in the forefront of your mind will help you to persevere through the difficult times so you can ultimately reach times of great prosperity and success, when you far exceed your sales quota.

I know a guy named Jon who manages a distribution center that stocks approximately 100 stores for The Home Depot. In a sense, he is in sales, and the stores are his customers. You can imagine what a complex job he has, receiving freight from planes, trains, and trucks, tracking his inventory, splitting it up to fulfill orders from stores, minimizing loss, managing employees, maintaining safety standards, handling documentation and paperwork, etc. He has many difficult days when he is on the phone for hours with technical support located in another country, fulfilling emergency orders of supplies for stores located in areas affected by natural disasters, or when another distribution center manager has a medical emergency, leaving him to manage both locations with little or no notice.

Jon has worked for The Home Depot for about twenty years, since he was in high school, and has worked his way up the ladder to his current position. You may ask yourself, what provides him with his motivation and perseverance? Does the company pay him extremely well, or does he have excellent perks and benefits that go along with his position? While he is compensated well for the work he does, has opportunities to earn bonuses, and has a full benefits package, he also has something else. Around the same time he began working at The Home Depot as a teenager, he also began dating a girl who is now his wife. The two of them decided they wanted her to be a stay-at-home mother to their children. They have a strong faith in the spiritual teachings of Jesus Christ, and they have made their relationship with God and their family the top priorities in all their decision making.

This has a profound effect on Jon's motivation and perseverance on the job. He always keeps in mind who and what he cares deeply about and works diligently to maintain his priorities and excellence. He knows he needs to meet all of the professional responsibilities of his position at work to achieve bonuses and meet all of his personal responsibilities at home.

It doesn't matter what your motivation is. It could be family, faith, financial obligations such as student loans or a mortgage, or the fact you're single and the only person who pays your bills. You need to identify your responsibilities and keep them in mind as you persevere through difficult times.

In contrast to Jon in the preceding example, I know another guy who has very few personal responsibilities. He doesn't have a family to take care of. He lives rent free in his friend's house that's about to be foreclosed by the bank. He has no bills to speak of. You might think this sounds great! No bills and no obligations! However, he also has no motivation. He has never been able to maintain a job with any employer for any length of time. He is now struggling to start up his own home improvement and remodeling company. However, because he has no personal responsibilities holding him accountable, there is a greater probability he will do a poor job of taking basic instructions, understanding the value and foundation of basic instructions, and managing his time, materials, finances, and professional responsibilities.

What is really being challenged when you don't meet your quota for a job you agreed to, chose and have an interest in performing as expected? In tough times, when you don't achieve your goals, or you feel management is persecuting you, sometimes you get offended.

BECOME RESPONSIBLE, BE ACCOUNTABLE

Accountability - The state of being accountable; liable to be called on to render an account; the obligation to bear the consequences for failure to perform as expected.

Be accountable. Perhaps you said something unprofessional to or about a coworker at the end of a long day. Even if the other person was not very respectful to you, you are responsible for yourself. Whatever you do or how you respond, you are responsible for your actions. You are always responsible for how you respond. Your behavior must always be under your control.

Every experience you encounter during difficult times **comes to challenge what you believe at your core**. Your decisions in adverse times will expose your hidden secrets. For example, if you fail to meet your sales quota for the month or a few months in a row, your response will reveal much about you. Do you make excuses or blame others? Do you blame the sales territory, products, sales process, or work conditions? Do you quit trying or develop a negative attitude?

All of these responses existed in you all along, and the adversity of not meeting your goal prompted you to expose your preexisting beliefs. Prior to working in your current position, you probably responded to adversity in the same way, but none of your coworkers or customers were aware of it because they didn't know you then. If you want to improve or achieve greater success than you ever have in the past, you need to make a conscious decision to handle adversity in a better manner. Here are some actions you can decide to take in advance when adversity inevitably strikes.

- **Stop blaming**. It is easy to blame others. In fact, you can find fault with or build a case against anyone. However, blaming others will not help you become responsible. Instead of pointing the finger, ask yourself what you could have done differently. You are always the person who controls what comes out of your mouth and what actions you take.

- **Acknowledge what happened if you make a mistake**. When you acknowledge, "Yes, I forgot to follow up at 3 p.m.," you eliminate the need to make up excuses. "I am very sorry," is the responsible four-word sentence, and when followed with, "Will you please give me another chance to correct this for you?" it helps customers who may be willing to forgive.

- **Accentuate the positive**. Words are the most powerful force in this world. The folks who blame are creating their world with their words. Move through your day with positive words. Have you ever noticed that people who don't take responsibility for their words and actions are negative and critical? If you make a commitment not to let your words speak against what you believe, you will be more likely to walk into the promises of what you believe will come to pass.

- **See yourself clearly**. Taking responsibility means acknowledging both your weaknesses and strengths. It means acknowledging all the areas you believe you're proficient in as well as the areas you aren't. When you take responsibility, you know your potential. You focus your energy on identifying areas for improvement and taking action to improve in those areas.

TRIALS AND TRIBULATIONS WHEN TAKING RESPONSIBILITY

You will experience trials and tribulations as you commit yourself to excellence in sales. However, don't act as though something strange is happening to you. Know that trials come not against you (the person), but to challenge what you truly believe in and are committed to. When you see these challenges in a positive light, you can count it all joy when you are faced with various trials and tribulations. The testing of your beliefs and goals will work your patience. Your patience must be exercised within you for you to show growth. This is a process, and it will not happen overnight. The testing of your faith means that what you believe will come to pass will be challenged. But let patience play itself out in your trials. Patience, hard work, and remaining focused will allow you to experience three advantages along the way:

1. You will gain knowledge or revelation about what is really happening.
2. You will gain better understanding about yourself in the situation you are dealing with.
3. You will gain wisdom on how to better manage a similar trial the next time you experience it.

These three improvements will allow you to be made perfect and complete by your trials and tribulations, complete and wanting nothing.

CHAPTER THREE

UNDERSTANDING

Happy is the man that finds wisdom, and the man that gets understanding. For the merchandise of it is better than the merchandise of silver and the gain there of than fine gold. Understanding is more precious than rubies: and all the things thou canst desire are not to be compared unto her. Proverbs 3:13-15

UNDERSTAND THE DREAM AND THE DREAMER INSIDE OF YOU

One Tuesday evening during the summer before I entered the tenth grade, my neighbor, a junior in high school, invited me to a high school basketball game to see Len Bias of Northwestern High School play basketball. The person who I was sitting with at halftime introduced me to Coach Mike Pearson, the football coach of the high school I would be attending the following year. Coach Pearson pulled me aside and asked me if I was thinking about coming to his school next year. I said I was. He looked me square in the eye with a dead stare and said, "You have good size for a 9th grader. If you can get good grades, work hard and do well on the field, you can get a college football scholarship."

This was one of the brightest days of my life. It was the first time someone meeting me for the first time, without knowing my background, gave me a compliment and helped me understand what I could become. Looking back, this was the first time the understanding/wisdom principle was introduced into my life.

How was the principle being introduced? First, I had to hear instructions. Then I had to understand what I heard. Finally, I had to be willing to do what I understood needed to be done to achieve my desired outcome. Over the next six months, I worked on gaining a better understanding from Coach Pearson of what was required to make the varsity football team. Then I needed to understand what was required to qualify for a Division One football scholarship.

After playing on the varsity football team for three years, I earned a Division One football scholarship. What was the lesson I learned at an early age? There are three things required to realize the goals you believe you can achieve in your life:

1. You must hear what is required for you to obtain your goal.
2. You must understand the requirements.
3. You must take the actions you now understand will lead to your goal.

THE GREATEST TRAGEDY YOU CAN EXPERIENCE IN LIFE

The greatest tragedy in life is to hear something, understand it, and not act on your knowledge. I've met people all over the world, and I often ponder what seeds were sown in their lives to produce the harvest they are living with physically, mentally, and spiritually. These thoughts challenge me to interrogate my choices and identify what I have heard and understood but have yet to commit to doing differently. Do you feel the same way sometimes?

I am a person who enjoys a healthy lifestyle. I eat healthy foods, exercise and feed my inner man information that builds up my spirit. I've found a steady balance is key to mental, spiritual and physical growth. This is something sales professionals must keep in mind.

Last year I went to the doctor because I was experiencing headaches at the end of the day. I found out I had high blood pressure and high cholesterol. While I looked great on the outside, the tests revealed I was a walking stroke risk.

The doctor stated he'd seen more young people dying from strokes due to high blood pressure and high cholesterol in the past three years than in the rest of his thirty years in practice. I sat in his office in disbelief. I never considered myself a person who was at risk for a stroke. My blood pressure was 189/125, and my cholesterol was over 220. The doctor couldn't believe I hadn't had a stroke. I left the doctor's office with full understanding of what I needed to do to bring my blood pressure and cholesterol down. I had a serious, life-changing decision to make based upon the following information:

1. I needed to understand my present condition.
2. I needed to understand the benefits and alternative outcomes to the actions I could take to change my present condition.

3. I needed to decide to do what I understood needed to be done to correct my present condition.

The doctor put me on blood pressure and cholesterol medication. The following day, I got my prescriptions filled. I also went back to the gym, walked outside daily, rode my bike, and focused on eating a mostly plant-based diet. Today, nine months later, the prescriptions are half of the original dosage and my blood pressure is only slightly higher than average.

WHY AM I SHARING THIS STORY?

On my first day of college, during summer football camp, I met my good friend for life, Terrance. Terrance was from Plainfield, New Jersey. We were both freshmen, registering for the first day of summer football camp. Terrance was a running back in college. He was 5 feet 9 inches tall and weighed 190 pounds, all muscle. Terrance was committed to always working out and eating healthy. One year the campus sponsored what they called "Campus Superlatives." Terrance was nominated as having the Best Body on Campus. One week later, the votes were tallied, and Terrance won "Mr. Body," the male with the best body on campus. I, on the other hand, was 6 feet 1 inch tall and weighed 205 pounds, and it was my goal to get up to 240 pounds. I was an offensive lineman and needed the extra pounds to compete for the starting position on the varsity college football team's offensive line.

Terrance and I played football for the next few seasons, both reaching our goals as First Team All-Conference football players. After college, Terrance went on to work at the water company in New Jersey. At least once a week for the past 27 years, I would talk with Terrance and reminisce over some of the funny stories. In his words, he was the very conservative roommate, and I was the risk taker, Frank the Tank.

Ten years ago, Terrance shared with me that he really needed to start working out because of all the stress on his job. He mentioned he had gained 80 pounds and had not been taking care of himself. He also said his doctor told him his blood pressure was very high and he needed to get on medication, change his eating habits, and lose weight in order to bring down his blood pressure.

Four months later, Terrance's wife called me and told me Terrance had a stroke at 2 a.m. and was in a coma. I couldn't believe it. I thought that when he came out of the coma in a few days, he would start taking his medication and get back on his exercise routine. Terrance was in intensive care for several weeks and showed signs of recovering. However, he got an infection in the brain and never recovered. He passed away on December 14, 2010 at only 45 years old.

I hadn't seen Terrance much during the last few years of his life. What I learned when he had the stroke was that he had not acted upon the understanding of what would be his outcome if he did not change his lifestyle. He didn't start exercising, taking his medication regularly, eating healthier, or losing weight when the doctor made those recommendations to him. In fact, he had gained even more weight. Witnessing this tragedy made me become even more committed to acting upon my understanding of my current condition, so my outcome would be different.

In my opinion, this was an unnecessary event, and has really made me reflect upon my understanding in all aspects of my life, including work and sales.

So ask yourself, what is it in your life that you understand but aren't acting on? That's what's stopping you from being the best in sales in your region. Are there personal issues you're dealing with that need to change to improve your present condition? Are you reluctant to take the necessary steps to bring about the desired outcome?

I've learned you have to resolve problems in your life. Problems don't go away on their own; they must be addressed, with the intent to resolve them. When your focus is on excellence, you have no space in your mind for thoughts which don't build you up or support your efforts in the field you've chosen.

HOW DO YOU IMPROVE YOUR UNDERSTANDING?

Effective listening is a vital part of gaining better understanding. The number one personal characteristic necessary to become a top producing salesperson is the ability to listen effectively. Don't be the salesperson who doesn't seek to understand before speaking on a matter; be the salesperson who listens to understand.

SIX WAYS TO IMPROVE YOUR LISTENING SKILLS

1. Leave your agenda at the front door and pick up the customer's agenda.
2. Give verbal and nonverbal cues that you're listening: head nods, supportive words, e.g. "I understand." "Good point." "Good idea." "Great thought."

3. Don't interrupt the customer when he or she is speaking. Once they finish, wait two seconds before you speak. The silence will always create a void, and the customer will share additional information.

4. Listen intently to what the customer is saying. When you want to get better clarification, ask who, what, when, where, why, or how?

5. Take notes with the details regarding the discussion. Especially detail items regarding follow up issues, timelines and dates. Write the details so you can review these items with your customer before you leave the meeting.

6. Never attempt to finish a sentence for a prospective customer. This is rude and is a clear sign you're not listening.

CHAPTER FOUR

SALESMANSHIP

Salesmanship: the practice of investigating and satisfying customer needs through a process that is efficient, fair, sincere, mutually beneficial, and aimed at a long-term productive relationship.

The difference between good salespeople and great ones is staggering. Good reps hit their quota most of the time; great reps have blow-out months or quarters, surpassing their quota. Good reps earn their prospects' trust and respect; great reps earn their prospects' admiration, loyalty, and referrals. Good reps can skillfully handle objections; great reps preemptively surface concerns and make them disappear.

If you want greatness, good news. Following these 17 rules of good sellers will help you become one of the top-selling salespeople on your team, or even at your company.

SELLING HABITS OF EFFECTIVE REPS

1) **They are committed to understanding their customers' requirements.** A clearly defined buyer has requirements whether they realize it or not. This is crucial to an effective sales process. A sales rep who

will drop their agenda to better understand the requirements of their customer is in the best position to meet or exceed the customers' expectations with their products or services. This will allow the representative to best evaluate if the prospect is a good fit. More information on understanding your customers' requirements can be found in Chapter Three: Understanding.

2) **Their sales process has no missteps.** High performing sales professionals have a laser focus on engaging customers. Once the discussion begins, the excellent sales professional will ask engaging questions to understand the following: the background of the organization; the contacts' journey to be in the present position; the impact of the current challenges not being met; how the current solution was put in place; who was involved, and; who has to be involved to initiate a new solution. Great sales people understand and track each and every one of these questions. They know the status and players involved in every prospective deal. For more information on performing this needs analysis, please see Chapter Seven: Needs Analysis.

3) **They become product experts.** You can't sell what you don't know. You must understand the products you're selling and how they fit the customers' requirements. Most importantly, becoming a product expert allows you to build trust and show integrity. It positions you be able to present products or solutions which demonstrate you've researched the customers' needs to recommend and demonstrate the "best fit" solution for them. Further instructions on how to

become an effective product expert can be found in Chapter Seven: Needs Analysis.

4) **They execute with diligence every day.** Effective sales reps combine a strategic plan, persistence, and timely execution with a goal to meet or exceed the customers' expectations. Diligence is discussed in further detail in Chapter Ten: Diligence.

5) **They establish trust with their buyers.** Buyers like to do business with people they trust. Often, trust is mistakenly overlooked or taken for granted. Sales professionals can be completely unaware of its value. It's important to form and cultivate effective relationships with your coworkers and customers for support, advice and/or approval. See Chapter One: Trust for a more in-depth discussion of how trust assists in producing sales.

6) **They practice effective listening.** Successful salespeople listen with a sincere attempt to understand. This is the first step to building a trusting relationship with your coworkers and customers. You can learn more about effective listening in Chapter One: Trust.

7) **They take full responsibly.** Responsibility is taking care of your obligations in an acceptable timeframe, maintaining accountability for your actions, and always preserving your trustworthiness. Learn how to take responsibility in Chapter Two: Responsibility.

8) **They realize objections, trials and tribulations are coming to test what they believe.** Your words are the true litmus test of what you believe. They share your beliefs with the world. The field of sales will require

you to make commitments with your mouth. Great salespeople don't say things contrary to what they believe, no matter how challenging times get. Read more about how to respond to being tested in Chapter 5: Tested.

9) **They are compelling storytellers.** Buyers don't want to hear a boring recitation of the features of your product or service. Good salespeople know this and weave the product or service they're selling into a larger story that shares examples of other customers who had similar experiences. This gives the salesperson credibility and allows the prospective customer to see through the eyes of a prospect who said yes to your solution. It also gives the prospect confidence your solution has the potential to resolve their problems. Most importantly, they don't have to feel like they are the first to say yes to the solution. I discuss the art of storytelling more in Chapter Five: Tested.

LIFE HABITS OF EFFECTIVE REPS

10) **They love what they do.** In sales, activity is often correlated with results. Ask a top salesperson what he really loves about selling and he'll say, "Everything." Being around them is similar to opening day of a new theme park. Their positive outlook and faith in the value of their profession ignites an attitude of excitement in others. It's clear to see they love what they do.

11) **They are Resourceful.** A successful sales rep needs to be resourceful. This is especially important when

reaching out to and prospecting for potential customers. This means going above and beyond using standard resources to close the deal. Thinking outside the box with patience will reveal the options impatience takes away.

12) **They get eight hours of sleep every night.** According to the American Academy of Sleep Medicine, most adults' need seven or eight hours a sleep per night. If you get less, you'll suffer from a laundry list of ailments, including:

- Irritability
- Decreased motivation
- Anxiety
- Symptoms of depression
- Reduced energy
- Fatigue
- Restlessness
- Poor decision making
- Increased errors
- Forgetfulness

MOTIVATION HABITS OF EFFECTIVE REPS

13) **They believe in what they're selling.** It's easier to be passionate about--and sell--a product when you genuinely believe in it. The best and most charismatic salespeople believe in themselves, their company and their product or service. They know they are the best. Confident salespeople act fearlessly and are willing to take calculated risks without worrying about hearing a "no" from the prospective customer.

14) **They're strongly motivated.** It doesn't matter what drives a salesperson, they need to be motivated. Every top salesperson has a burning reason for showing up to work every day and giving it their all. Perhaps they want to buy a house and must make at least 110% of their quota every month to do so. Maybe they're super competitive and always want to be at the top of the leaderboard. Maybe they need to prove to themselves they can do well in sales.

Ask yourself, *"What's my #1 reason for wanting to be successful?"* If you can't immediately come up with an answer, you need to find that motivator.

15) **They view their customers' success as their own.** Top reps don't stop working when the prospect signs on the dotted line. Instead, they touch base with their customers frequently to seek feedback and provide tactical suggestions.

16) **They constantly build personal relationships.** A great sales professional is always listening subconsciously with their internal ear to discern whether the person they are speaking with has the potential to assist them in their line of business at some point in the future.

17) **They prepare ahead of time.** An effective salesperson preplans before every call. This means they do research on their prospect and gather information before meeting with a customer.

The best reps never wing it. They go in with a well thought out plan and a contingency plan. They anticipate challenges or questions and prepare effective responses to objections to avoid losing the sale.

CHAPTER FIVE
TESTED

"In sales everything you believe makes you
successful will be tested."

Those who say they can sell are correct. Those who say they can't sell are correct. In the field of sales, these two statements are both true. Your words are the magic ingredients framing and creating your world.

My job is to challenge you to establish your foundation. By using your words to make better decisions outside of your sales jobs, you will build a solid foundation from which to make the best decisions when you're selling.

THE FORCE OF FEAR IS COMING TO CHALLENGE WHAT YOU BELIEVE

Fear will come to challenge what you really believe. It will wage a war for your mind. Fear is defined in Webster's dictionary as an unpleasant, often strong emotion caused by anticipation or awareness of danger; an instance of this emotion, or a state marked by this emotion.

WHAT RESPONSES CAN FEAR TRIGGER IN YOU?

Fear is a powerful and primitive emotion. The fear response arises from the perception of danger. It serves a critical function in keeping organisms alive. Fear in human beings may occur in response to a specific stimulus occurring in the present, or in anticipation or expectation of a future threat perceived as a risk to body or life. The responses triggered by fear can be divided into two groups: emotional and biochemical. The biochemical response is universal, while the emotional response is highly individualized.

BIOCHEMICAL REACTION

The biochemical reaction to fear is an automatic response. It is most likely an evolutionary development. When we confront a perceived danger, our bodies respond in specific ways. Physical reactions include sweating, increased heart rate, and high levels of adrenaline. This physical response is sometimes known as the "fight or flight" response. The sole purpose of these reactions is to provide the body with the energy to either enter combat or to run away. In other words, its purpose is to ready us to act. Once we act, **fear** is pointless.

EMOTIONAL RESPONSE

The emotional response to fear is highly personalized. Although the physical reaction is the same, fear may be perceived as either positive or negative. Most individuals develop a conditioned emotional response to feelings of fear:

> *The conditioned emotional response, specifically here the conditioned fear response, is an emotional response that*

results from classical conditioning, usually from the association of a relatively neutral stimulus with a painful or fear-inducing experience.

Others have a negative reaction to the feeling of fear, avoiding fear-inducing situations at all cost.

THREE WAYS TO OVERCOME THE FEAR OF FAILURE

1. **Renew your mind daily**. Renewing your mind is one of the surest ways to overcome your fears and develop the courage needed to get to where you want to go. Develop affirmations that build you up. Visualizing where your life is heading will increase your self-confidence. Read uplifting books to renew your mind daily with positive thoughts. This will help stop the negative inner dialogue going on in your mind. Remember, faith comes by hearing and so does fear. If you don't take the time to intentionally renew your mind with positive thoughts, the pressures of life, obstacles you're faced with, and disappointments will produce fear, doubt, and unbelief.

2. **Excuses are the tools of the incompetent.** Let your "yes" mean "yes" and your "no" mean "no." Stop making excuses for unfinished tasks you commit to. Come out of the middle of being undecided. Being undecided will often lead to complacency or procrastination. Once you have committed to a task, complete the task. If you're not sure you want to commit fully to a task, don't sign up for it. Prevent

unfinished tasks from accruing on the front end. You'll have less excuses and see more success with completing tasks. Remember, it's your integrity that's on the line for the things you commit to. I once received a 4 out of 10 on a performance review. That year I was 140% of plan. My manager sat me down and shared with me that while I was a great salesman, I was the worst person on the team when it came to getting my administrative paperwork in on time. All I could come up with were excuses for not being compliant. I never thought of my lack of being compliant with expense reports, monthly sales reports, and other administrative expectations as a concern because I was meeting my monthly numbers. I pondered my manager's comments and my performance review for one solid week. I decided this was something I could control and change. I decided to meet with my administrator to evaluate her perception of me and attempt to understand how my lateness in turning in paperwork impacted her job. I also wanted to understand how other team members were staying on top of their administrative expectations. I was determined to make administrative details one of my strongest attributes. The following year I received a 10 out of 10 for my performance review.

3. Make failure a tool for future success. For most people, the fear of not knowing is they reason they will fail. On your success journey, failure is an inevitable part of success. Once you realize this, it will allow you to be better prepared to overcome this fear along the way. Failure can become a vital key to your future success once you learn to evaluate, understand, and implement new strategies to prevent each failure. Everyone has experienced the fear of failure. The key is to capture every thought or imagination that comes against your dreams. You must take hold of these negative thoughts which come to only to kill, steal, and destroy the greatness within you. Write these thoughts down and identify them as fear.

Keep the mindset "I am planting good seeds that will produce a great harvest. I will grow mature, achieve perspective, and realize the pain of failure or obstacles can be a valuable, necessary part of my journey."

Seeds are usually small; some are even tiny. Despite their small size, though, seeds contain all the materials necessary to sprout to life as a plant. When seeds are planted, they first grow roots. Once these roots take hold, a small plant will begin to emerge and eventually break through the soil. When this happens, we say the seed has sprouted. The scientific name for this process is called germination. As the plant grows and begins to make its own food from nutrients it takes from the soil, it will grow into a larger plant. The seed itself is like a survival package. It contains the food the seed needs while it is growing roots and forming into a small plant. The three things plants need to grow are light, food and water. Light, whether from the sun or an artificial light source like a light bulb, gives the small plant the energy it needs to begin photosynthesis. Photosynthesis is the process the plant uses to convert light energy into food.

Remember your positive words/visual affirmations are SEEDS. The words spoken daily over your life, goals, and objectives become the light and water needed for the seeds to grow.

"YOUR WORDS ARE THE TRUE LITMUS TEST OF WHAT YOU BELIEVE"

Consistency in the field you've chosen will require you to make a commitment with your mouth that you won't let your works speak anything contrary to what you believe. This will be the most powerful affirmation you will make in this industry. This commitment will not come without a concentrated effort and daily practice. Your words are creating the world you will live in tomorrow. I suggest you take the following steps to build the world of sales accomplishments you're attempting to believe for:

1. **Frame your world with your words.** Get a picture frame large enough to write in. Identify all the things in life you believe your sales' efforts will provide for you and write them in the frame.

2. **Call things that are not as though they were in existence.** You must begin training your mind to call things that are not as though they already exist. Confess daily what things are coming into your life daily by your faith and confession. You will be responsible for holding fast to each confession of faith

in the things you are believing and working for. If you will not give up, in due season you shall reap a harvest. Keep your efforts focused on confessing what you're believing for. Faith will come by hearing yourself say these things.

3. **Never use your words to confess the present challenging condition**. When you believe for excellence, all your words and energy must be focused on building faith in what you believe. Faith comes by hearing, but so does fear. If you keep stating what your present condition is, your practices and behaviors will follow what you are saying. You will notice your problems will become bigger than the positive vison you're working toward. If you say, "I will never make my sales number," you will never achieve those numbers. You will gain more faith in the problem than in your vision. The problem will be bigger than your faith in the promise.

4. **Surround yourself with other sales professionals who have made a commitment.** Identify the best sales professionals in your company and learn their practices. The words and daily practices of these individuals will remain in alignment.

5. **Write out a detailed action plan quarterly that defines what activities are required of you daily to walk into the promises you are confessing and believing in.**

THE PRINCIPLE OF CALLING THINGS THAT ARE NOT AS THOUGH THEY WERE

This principle was established thousands of years ago and is practiced everyday. Whether you have parents, pets, grandparents, aunties, uncles, or kids, whether you believe in God or play the lottery, the principle doesn't change. How does this principle work?

One will speak or confess an event that has not occurred at the time of the confession. The confession brings about the desired result. Often when I share this with sales professionals, they look at me as though I've completely lost my mind. This principle doesn't work just because you say something. However, stating it will be the core ingredient to bringing forth the harvest in your life. Let's look at a few examples of this principle at work in our daily practices:

- Your pet dog Cooper is outside in the backyard, and he is not in sight. You say, "here Cooper, Cooper, Cooper," even though you can't see him. All of a sudden, Cooper appears.

- Your daughter Lisa is outside playing with her friends out of your view. You open the back door and call out to her, "Lisa, it's time to come in. Dinner's ready." Lisa hears your voice, responds, and eventually appears.

- The bible says in the beginning there was darkness and God spoke the words "let there be light." God used words to change conditions.

- Daily lottery/Casinos: Prior to the lottery, one has to make predictions and pick numbers to play before the cut off deadline. People use their words to call the numbers they are hoping for into existence prior to the event occurring.

In all these instances, the principle of using your words to call things that are not as though they were has been employed. I've used this principle for over 20 years to bring forth a great manifestation of excellence in the field of sales. You are empowered to exercise these same practices for yourself. This will not be easy to do. A made-up mind is required to accomplish this task. You will need to exercise a heightened awareness of the speaking patterns of those in your inner circle.

Once your mind is made up, you must pay close attention to those in your inner trust circle who are speaking negative words. Their words represent unbelief. You must decide whether you're going to assist them in identifying what those words represent. I'm not saying walk up to a complete stranger and attempt to correct their speech. What I'm suggesting is you are entitled to evaluate if those you've chosen to invite into your personal space should continue to stay in your inner circle.

Share your intention to accomplish your goals by creating with your words with those close to you. For example, say "I am creating my world with my words." This may create a make or break situation in some of your professional relationships. Those who can understand what you're attempting to accomplish in life will be happy to support your vision. They will attempt to change their words to change their world and join in your quest to excel in working toward a vision.

Those who think you are crazy will be a test challenging your commitment to what you say you believe. In your pursuit of excellence, the disbelief of others will evoke emotional pain. You will experience persecution and feel afflicted at times for your beliefs. Don't feel as though this is strange. This has not come against you personally; this challenge has come about to test what you say you believe. If you pass the test, you will find you've grown in these areas. If a person's unbelief or confessing their doubt is stronger than what you believe, there's a strong possibility you will fall victim to their influence. You, my friend, will have to take this test over and over again until you overcome these obstacles on the road to excellence. You must decide to what extent you are going to value this relationship.

I have made a conscious decision to spend my time with people who are motivated and inspired to have a well-balanced life and become the best they can be in life. Sales is hard enough without surrounding yourself with people who speak negativity into your world. Please don't confuse eliminating negativity with a lack of good counsel who may require you to be open to changing some behaviors that may be stifling your growth.

Speaking faith-filled words will produce the faith you need to accomplish the task. Your words are the pathway to your beliefs. Every challenge you experience in the field of sales or life comes to challenge what you believe. When will these challenges come? They will come when you are not making the numbers you're forecasted to make. You will start to feel pain, persecution or affliction internally.

WHAT'S BEING TESTED IN ME?

As an Account Representative, I received a call from a prospective customer who wanted to purchase $490,000.00 of Xerox Equipment. At that time, my monthly sales quota was $24,000.00 a month. Receiving this call and closing this deal would have made me a star. I picked up the phone and called the prospective customer back. The customer was Transunion Company, located in Delaware. The customer proceeded to share what he was interested in purchasing with me. He said he was working with three organizations, and the one which gave him the best deal would be the company he chose. I assured him that he was working with the best company and that I would get him all the information he needed to make the best decision.

Little did I know the surprise I had in store. The customer ended up being the CFO for the company.

He shared his request for 26 Xerox machines with me over the phone. Each of the machines he was requesting was going to a different part of the new building they were in the process of constructing. Each machine had to be configured with the proper accessories to accommodate departmental needs. We started our discussion running the numbers based on his request for very specific machine configurations at 9 am. The customer's request changed 15 times over the course of the day, from the requested units to the machine configurations. Each time a change was requested by the customer, he asked if I would send over the new proposed monthly totals for the request. I was feeling overloaded with the requests and constant changes. We typically had a finance manager I was assigned to work with; however, our finance manager was out of the office on this day. I was the only one working through every scenario. After 6 hours of working on this project for the customer, the prospective customer called me and said "Virgil, you sound like you may be a great guy, however, I have put together a spreadsheet of every scenario you've given me today. I notice you're very inconsistent with your leasing figures and your service rates. Therefore, I've made my decision to select another vendor to meet our needs. Thank you for all your help." Then he disconnected the call.

Needless to say, I was in shock. I went back to my desk, startled over what had just happened. Disappointed, confused, and upset were just a few of the emotions I was feeling. This transaction bothered me for several weeks. I'd really thought I was exceptional at understanding customer requirements and closing sales. I was especially upset about the impact this could've had on exceeding my monthly sales quota. Pondering this scenario for weeks to come, I decided to commit myself to preparing to be in the best possible position so this outcome never happened again. I realized I wasn't very good at working numbers for customers quickly and efficiently. I made it a personal challenge to meet weekly with our financial analyst to understand how he worked and came up with financial packages for customers. I was determined to be an expert for my customer. This gave me great confidence and the ability to understand and memorize financial options for the customers I was meeting with. This became an awesome weapon. I finished the year at 220% of my sales plan.

HOW DO YOU ESCAPE THE FEAR OF FAILURE AGAIN?

I came up with this acronym to use every time I lost a sale. Going through this cycle helps me improve and be in the best position to avoid repeating the same mistakes. If you take your sales profession as seriously as I do, in your quest to be excellent, you will find value in this process as well.

E.S.C.A.P.E

E. Evaluate: Evaluate the evidence of fear. Is the evidence which appears real actually real? People are by nature afraid of change. They fear change will somehow disrupt their lives or uproot them from their comfort zone. But change serves to transport us into new, greater manifestations of ourselves. Allow necessary changes to come your way, even if they may seem frightening at first. Every instance of change can serve a purpose towards your highest good.

S. Selectivity: You must learn to be selective about what you want out of life and the things you pursue. Select a vision for your future and stick to your mental projection until you've brought it fully to life.

C. Commitment. Were my efforts, presentation, appearance, timeliness, listening skills, and material representative of a commitment to excellence every time I met with the customer?

A. Accountability. Was the information I presented accurate? Was the information presented in the absolute best way it could have been? Was I prepared with the correct information during each encounter with the customer? Did I preplan the sales call to the best of my ability? Did I follow up on every item I committed to do, and did I do so on time?

P. Patience. How patient was I when attempting to understand what the customer was requesting? Did I really understand what they were asking of me? What was the quality of the information I prepared for the customer? Did I meet or exceed the customers' expectations?

E. Emotionally. How am I feeling emotionally? Where did I feel like I may have lost my momentum in the sales cycle? What emotion(s) did the customer express that were overlooked or underserved? If you are going to shun fear forever, you must work on your self-esteem. Fear arises from not believing enough in your own abilities and talents. When you live in the mindset of "Why me? I can't do it" or, "I don't think I am good enough," you narrow your window of success to a slim opening and allow fear to grow within you.

WORDS ARE SEEDS

You are the sower who sows into this world by the words which come out of your mouth. Whatever results you have in the field of sales consistently is a direct result of your words and activities. No salesperson has a consistent surprise harvest.

CHAPTER SIX

INTEGRITY

Integrity:

1: firm adherence to a code of especially moral or artistic values

2: an unimpaired condition

3: the quality or state of being complete or undivided

SALES INTEGRITY

Integrity is a quality aspired to by every sales professional worth their weight. It encompasses many of the best and most admirable traits inside each one of us: honesty, uprightness, trustworthiness, fairness, loyalty, and the courage to keep one's word and one's promises regardless of the consequences. The word "integrity" is derived from the Latin word for wholeness and denotes a man who has successfully integrated good virtues into his character– one who not only speaks about integrity but demonstrates its characteristics by his actions.

Who are you when no one is looking? In a day, you have many opportunities to interact with family, friends, co-workers, and teammates. These relationships are a vital part of your life. The people in these groups get an up-close view of your true character.

Reflecting on all the years of sales I've experienced, I'm convinced it's what's on the inside of a person that drives them to excel and always desire to do and be the best. There are several internal components that are integral to lasting success. The one I will focus on in this chapter is integrity.

In college I had a friend who shared a simple test her mother used to give her friends when they visited. Her mom would leave a few dollars lying out in the open. The visitors didn't know her mom was monitoring the stashes to see if her friends would remove what she had placed there. I couldn't believe her mom would put her friends to the test. This got me thinking about other possible extreme measures people would utilize to monitor or measure the integrity of a person.

This lesson has remained with me for over 30 years. It's still as fresh in my mind as the day I heard this story. Why am I sharing this story with you? This was a valuable lesson for me at an early age. For the first time, I was aware of how someone else evaluated the integrity of others without the person being evaluated realizing it. There's a possibility everyone you meet has a testing measure to evaluate whether they will trust you.

During the time of the above lesson I was just starting my first sales job at Sears. I worked in the lawn and gardening department selling riding lawnmowers on commission. I was fortunate to work with three very different, mature salesmen who had different styles and backgrounds. Mr. Carter was a 66-year-old sales man who also owned the first African American restaurant in Dover

Delaware. He also was an insurance salesman who worked in the insurance industry for over 30 years. Mr. Carter wasn't a technical specialist, but he knew everyone in town since he had lived in Dover for over 40 years. I noticed the people who knew him connected with the steadfastness of his dedication and commitment to the community.

I realized this connection was earned and not given away. This, in fact, was another pillar of integrity. Once this was established with customers, I would watch him go to work. The sales cycle often moved from connection, to understanding what they were looking for, to finding the product, to a general overview, to closure quickly.

Mr. Carter's integrity kept him at the top of the sales chart month after month. His sales numbers were staggering. He was one of the top five performers within the region consistently.

Mr. Windsly was another top sales producer within the region for our store. Mr. Windsly was a retired military man who was always well dressed and well spoken. Mr. Windsly was our technical specialist. He knew every technical aspect there was to know about every riding lawnmower.

When a customer would come into the store and speak with me, I would begin explaining how a product worked and what separated our products from our competitors' models. Sometimes I would get stuck because I didn't have the correct information. I would run over to Mr. Windsly and ask him about the specs, and he would ask me "what does the specs manual say about your question?"

In the beginning, this would bother me because inside I knew it would be so simple for him to just answer the question, but he wouldn't. Being left to search for the answers myself, I learned I had to take responsibility for becoming an expert on the products if I wanted to become a top producer like Mr. Windsly.

You may ask what this has to do with integrity. This demonstrates another dimension of a salesman's integrity: taking his or her craft seriously. Basic knowledge of your product will get the customer interested. Detailed knowledge of the product will allow your customers to respect you. Exceptional knowledge of your product and your competition will allow your customers and prospective customers to consider you an expert resource they need to work with if they want to work with the best and buy the right product.

I realized product knowledge was another form of building the trust and integrity of every prospective customer. Not just for the first sale, but the second, third, and additional sales opportunities as well.

Integrity represents doing the job right the first time. As a marketing representative for Xerox, I was able to put up outstanding sales numbers month after month. I thought posting great numbers monthly would be all I needed to be looked upon as a superstar in the company. I came to realize integrity was not only measured by sales numbers, but also by your ability to perform the job right the first time in every area you serve within the company.

SEVEN STEPS TO BUILDING INTEGRITY AS A SALES PROFESSIONAL

1. **Maintain accurate records**. Don't fudge the numbers after a business trip or write off items unrelated to business as company entertainment. Don't guestimate your numbers. Write exact figures on an expense sheet instead of rounding up numbers to pocket a little extra reimbursement. Be sure to account for all personal or company expenses related to your job.

2. **Intend to change**. Once you have become conscious of how you rationalized yourself into doing something unethical, vow to change your behavior in that area.

3. **Check in with yourself**. Conduct a scan of your behaviors and actions regularly to see how you are doing. Many people go along day to day and don't take the time or effort to examine themselves.

4. **Keep your word**. Don't make promises you can't keep or lie about something you said or did. Even small white lies can be dangerous when exposed. Follow through when asked to do something, and don't blame others when mishaps occur. Take responsibility for your actions when things don't work out rather than resorting to excuses or half-truths.

5. **Help others**. Without being sanctimonious, help other people see when they have an opportunity to grow in integrity. Do this without blame or condemnation; instead, do it with love and helpfulness.

6. **Build your own internal trust so you can trust other people more**. To do this, it is important to follow the

ideas listed above. These ideas will allow you to move consciously in a direction of higher personal integrity.

7. **Break habits.** Many incorrect things you do are the result of bad habits. Expose your habits and ask if they are truly healthy for you.

LACK OF INTEGRITY TAKES ONE OF FOUR FORMS:

1. **Inconsistency between a person's words and actions** (saying one thing and doing another). Verbal inconsistency expresses itself as a lack of honesty.

2. **Inconsistency between one's actions and one's words and values.** This inconsistency comes across as a lack of courage to act according to his values.

3. **Inconsistency between one's values and one's words/actions.** This syndrome results from saying or doing what others want to please them.

4. **Inconsistency in every area**–no consistency or integrity among a person's values, words and actions. Such a person is out of touch with himself and reality; he is not functioning in the real world.

The common denominator in all these different forms of a lack of integrity is simple: inconsistency. We all have values we live by, whether we are conscious of them or not. Our values energize our motives, and our motives drive our actions. People with high integrity have high values and live by them.

CHAPTER SEVEN

NEEDS ANALYSIS

WHAT IS NEEDS ANALYSIS IN SELLING?

Whether we realize it or not, every person we encounter in our profession is walking around with needs they are looking to have met. When I was a General Sales Manager for General Motors brand vehicles, I would sit and watch customers come into the dealership. Other sales professionals would say these customers were out on the lot just kicking tires. Every time I would hear someone say this, I would think to myself, "this sales consultant doesn't value understanding the needs of the customer." Why would a customer have to drive all the way over to the dealership to kick our tires? There is always a reason and a story behind when a customer shows any interest in your products.

When a sales professional is completely incapable of strategically working backwards to understand how a prospective customer made the decision to express an interest in their products or services, one of two factors are in play. Either the sales professional is unaware of how to systematically extract the information from the prospective client, or they are clueless as to how to implement a strategy to best understand the background and experiences of the customer which created the interest in the salesman's product or service. In either case, the sales professional must master the art of effective listening and perfect the art of asking who, what, when, where, and how. Once trained in strategic questioning, these five interrogatives, along with patience in listening, will yield the salesman a great harvest of better understanding the customers' stories and the reasons they have an interest in his products or services.

Selling can be a difficult skill to learn. It's hard to cultivate the right formulas that work consistently. Each aspect of your selling process needs to be perfected by continuous feedback, often from a sales manager. Each sales professional has some area within the needs analysis framework they like to focus on because it's an area they are comfortable in. However, the most important part of the selling process—creating value for both you and the customer—is found in the results of your discovery questioning. This is what intense investigation preparation must offer. I like to think of this process as if I were a top paid defense attorney and my case depended on the evidence I uncovered in my needs analysis investigation.

I have adopted a base level for all needs analysis questioning to start. I like to work backwards with every prospective customer I meet, listening effectively to the customer's interests as I attempt to create a bridge from their interests to where they are today.

Often, I look around the client's office and study what's on their walls to identify areas of interest. This allows me to make a connection point with the customer's interests. Once I find this point of interest, I ask questions, working backwards to understand how a customer comes to be in the position they're in. How did they get into this position? Why are they looking for a car, financial advice, or a computer? This opens the door for me to begin understanding the circumstances, consequences, obstacles, motivations, pressures, or financial obligations, goals or objectives present and involved in their decisions. This will give me a much better feel for what is motivating my prospect to engage in discussions with me.

If you rush through this process, you run the risk of devaluing your prospect's story and showing disrespect for their journey. It will be very difficult for you get the sales process back on track and close the sale.

One of the first things I would recommend, and I believe this shows great integrity and honor, is to get yourself a good tablet for taking notes. This process is where you will build your case to close the sale. Think of yourself as a top defense attorney, building the case you're going to present to your customer with all the details and facts you've extracted from your needs analysis. You will present the facts of your case along with your proposal to earn the right to advance your sales cycle and work with them on your proposed solution.

1. **Identify the problems or situations**. This will allow you to hear what the customer views as current concerns. Next, focus on how these concerns impact what they're trying to accomplish. For example, what happens when deadlines aren't met? What cost is associated with not doing the job right the first time? How will this personally impact the prospect? Understand their criteria for decision making and answers to the following questions:

1) Challenges: What are the problems, challenges, impacts, or dissatisfactions? 2) Consequences: What is the implication of the problem?

You must take your time and write down all the information the customer shares in this area. This is the first step in building your case for them to do business with you.

2. **Review**. Reviewing your customer's concerns is critical. As you review each of the prospect's concerns, share each of them with the customers and get their agreement this is their concern. After you review the last concern, ask the prospect if they would be comfortable moving forward with you if you can show them solutions that will meet or exceed their expectations. Systematically addressing one area of concern at a time will allow you to earn credibility with the prospect. It is important to remember to build your case for why the prospect is going to make a clear, educated decision to do business with you. You're demonstrating you understand their requirements and are preparing to share with them the best options to meet their needs.

3. **Demonstration.** Frame your demonstration around the areas of concern you discovered in the needs analysis. This is where your ability to meet your customers' needs and solve the problem. This may require you involving your support team to create solutions which show your company can resolve/fix any issues and demonstrate your process and ability to customize a resolution.

At the beginning of each product demo, it is

important to review your customer's areas of concern. You want to do this to gain agreement from your customer. This is to solidify these items were in fact the basis for agreement when they agreed to allow you to present products or services you believe will meet their specific concerns. If you fail to set the tone for the demonstration, you may be giving your prospect a way out in the end. Remember, you're building a case for the customer with your demonstration to get them to say yes to doing business with you.

STEPS TO A POWERFUL PRODUCT DEMONSTRATION

1. **Know your product.** Take the time to become an expert on your products. You may want to work with a product specialist. Whatever it takes, become the expert. Before every demo, make sure you've given yourself adequate time to prepare and work through a live demo on your own or with the specialist. Make sure the product is working properly. You should feel comfortable with every feature the product offers and know what every button accomplishes, etc. Show how the product specifically meets the goals and objectives of the customer. Demonstrating your ability to meet the customers' needs will allow you to demonstrate your competency and increase your chances of closing the sale.

2. **Practice**. Practice the demonstration until you have mastered it based on your customer's specific needs. Manually go through each screen. Work on your timing. Check to see if the equipment needs service.

Consider outlining the process for the demonstration.

3. **Prepare.** Prepare to win the case you're presenting from the notes in your needs analysis. Arrive early. Set up your computer and/or projector with all connections. You must commit to this process to excel. The customer is taking their time to allow you to present your case. If you don't close the sale, it's because you have not valued the process and prepared with excellence.

4. **Start off by reiterating the goals of the meeting.** For example, your goals could be to get feedback, a contract, and/or referrals to other possible buyers. When you're ready to dive into the product itself, go slowly. Leave each page on the screen for a few extra seconds to allow enough time for your audience to read all the text. If you're using a computer, move the mouse slowly. Talk about the features as you show them. Pause and ask for questions at each juncture in the presentation. This also allows you the chance to take a sip of water!

5. **Afterwards, ask for questions.** If you know the audience is evaluating other products, ask a question like "Were you looking for something you didn't see?" or "Did you see anything that looked especially beneficial?" You always want to harvest some good feedback. When it seems like the meeting/demo is winding down, close the meeting by saying something like "Thanks again for your time. We're very interested in working with you /your company on implementing this product."

CHAPTER EIGHT

GOALS

IT'S IMPOSSIBLE TO HIT A TARGET YOU CAN'T SEE.

In sales, it is critical to have goals set for every stage of your day and sales career. Daily goals keep your day on track as much as career goals help you remember the purpose of your work and overcome the obstacles you will confront along your path.

How do you know whether you're progressing in your career? How can you determine whether you're getting better in your work? To lay out a path to success, you need to set goals--for the month, quarter, year, five years, and so on. Long-term goals provide big picture focus, while daily and weekly goals break down big picture goals into bite-sized, actionable items. As you regularly reach these goals, you can make your goals larger. This creates accurate data to measure your progress in your career.

Ayelet Fishbach from the University of Chicago and Melissa Ferguson from Cornell University produced a study around the social psychology of goals. They explain that goals "constitute the focal points around which human behavior is organized. Much of what people think about, feel, and do revolves around the goals they are trying to meet, or those goals they have already met or dismissed."

WHAT IS A GOAL? A STRETCH GOAL?

Selling products and services over the last 25 years as a top performer, I have noticed the foundation of how you see yourself is reflected in the goals, expectations and visions you establish for yourself. Without goals and vison in selling, you will fall into the dangerous category of those sales professionals who will not succeed.

DO YOU HAVE GOOD EYESIGHT BUT POOR VISION?

This means you see what's directly in front of you, but you have a hard time seeing the bigger picture. If your goals are only getting you through to the next hour, day or week, you may have poor vision. Have no fear; I can walk you through my process of goal-setting so you can better understand how to clarify your vision.

A goal is the object of a person's ambition or effort. Goals can make keeping your focus and motivation moving in a positive direction much easier. Fishbach and Ferguson lead off their study by defining a goal as "a cognitive representation of a desired endpoint that impacts evaluations, emotions and behaviors."

It's important to utilize goals in your professional life so you can measure your growth and ensure you're continuously developing along a positive trajectory. I recommend setting both a target and a stretch goal. Your target goal is one which is realistic for you to meet but not subpar. A stretch goal, or what I like to call your sales vision, is a goal you continue to work towards should you reach your target goal before your deadline. It'll be a little unrealistic, but the challenge will increase your motivation. This will keep you energized to push past your target goal and reach further than you ever thought you could!

HOW TO EFFECTIVELY SET GOALS

The biggest key when setting a goal is to make sure it is measurable and will lay the foundation for you to achieve your big picture plans. In 1981, George Doran presented SMART goals. SMART is a mnemonic device for the way in which it is best to establish goals.

S – **Specific.** If your goals aren't specific, then you won't be able to take clear action to achieve them.

This is your opportunity to define the goal with as much detail as possible. To plainly define your goal, answer as many of the following questions as you can with the information and forethought you have:

What are you working to accomplish?

Who is involved in achieving this goal?

Where will you be doing this work?

Why are you working on this goal?

- This is the most important question as it gives you the opportunity to fully understand the purpose and reasons for working toward this goal.

Which constraints or resources do you have?

- By thoroughly answering this question, you can map out potential roadblocks while also understanding the resources you have available as you work toward your goal.

M – **Measurable.** This is how you'll know when your goal

is reached. It's important to associate numbers with your goals so you can track your progress as you work.

This is when you lay out your "how." How much? How many? How will you know when you've reached your goal?

For example, if you have a sales quota this month to sell 25% more than you did last month, use this opportunity to analyze your process. Do you cold call? How many meetings with potential clients do you have set up? Can you schedule 25 or even 50 percent more? Can you increase the number of product demonstrations you perform by 25%? What about 50%?

Understanding the numbers around your goal and your process will give you guidance as you work toward reaching your goals each month, quarter, or year.

A – Attainable. Has a supervisor ever set a goal for you and you thought "there is no way I can achieve this in the allotted time"? What about being a little overly ambitious and setting a goal just out of reach for you given your resources and time? It didn't feel great when you missed the mark, did it?

If you constantly set goals too far out of reach, then you will get discouraged in your work. However, you also don't want your goals to be below the expected standard of work. If you highly surpass your goal each month, while it may feel nice, it's clear you could set your bar a little higher to create motivation and room for growth.

I previously mentioned setting what I call stretch goals. These goals are less likely to be attainable in the timeframe you have set up. However, as you start to develop your time management skills and plan your actions with strong intentions, you can grow and expand to match these goals, making goals that once seemed unattainable, attainable.

R – Relevant. There must be a clear reason for achieving this goal. You must be working toward a higher purpose, whether it's providing for your family, saving for a new house, or planning your next step in your career as a salesman. By having your goals remain relevant to your purpose, you will maintain your motivation to reach them.

I like to set what I call foundational goals. You achieve this goal to lay the foundation to have or do something more in the future. If your goal doesn't link to a higher purpose or open up opportunities for you in other avenues, then it can be easy to lose focus and forget why you even set the goal in the first place.

T – Timely. There needs to be an ending or set time for when the goal needs to be reached. Without deadlines there is no accountability.

Without a deadline, there is no sense of urgency. There is nothing to say if you've truly reached your goal. Anything can be done with endless amounts of time, but what can be done this week? This month? This year?

This can also help develop your skills around time management. When you are prompted to reach a deadline, such as with an assignment from a supervisor, can prioritize your to-do list and ensure every action you take is an intentional move toward reaching the goal you have in place.

WHAT HAPPENS WHEN YOU DON'T REACH YOUR GOALS?

Are you facing a corrective action plan or termination?

In sales, your supervisors will help set goals for you. Your company may set quarterly or monthly goals every salesperson must reach. If you consistently fail to reach these goals, there's generally an action plan spread out over a course of time, usually 90 days, to see if you can change your habits and better reach the goals in front of you.

I have been on a corrective action plan a time or two, and while it may cause panic, it's the most important time to stay calm and get focused.

Dopamine is the neurotransmitter chemical in your brain associated with a feeling of pleasure. When you reach your goals, your brain rewards you by releasing a large dose of dopamine. However, when you do not reach your goals, your brain can also respond as a cruel punisher. When your supervisor says you may be facing termination, cortisol, the stress chemical, begins to flow in tidal waves through your brain.

When you set a goal, your brain looks at it as a prized possession. Thus, when you don't reach it, your brain will cut off your supply of dopamine, which may trigger feelings like anxiety, fear, or sadness.

Fishbach and Ferguson said, "goals, and the ways in which people pursue them, also determine people's evaluations, moods, and emotional experiences both during a pursuit and after a pursuit has been completed or abandoned."

Not reaching goals is a part of growth. When you don't meet a goal you've set, it's an opportunity to open a dialogue with yourself, a mentor, or supervisor. This is your chance to discuss what happened, why goals weren't reached, and analyze opportunities to make sure the goals are met next time.

TRAITS AND SKILLS FOR REACHING GOALS

Focus and environment are the two most important skills you need to reach your goals once they are intentionally and effectively set.

Focus is the number one trait you need to maintain to reach your goals. To better focus, you need to stop multitasking and try different working styles. By tackling tasks one at a time, you're able to finish them faster and generally with a higher quality. This allows you to remain more focused while completing the task.

It may seem easier to tackle busy work such as responding to emails first to get it out of the way instead of diving into more difficult work. However, your brain needs to be stimulated in the morning to get the most work done. By tackling a bigger, more creative task, your brain gets the boost it needs.

A great way to stay focused and tackle the bigger tasks is to time block your schedule. When time blocking your schedule, you have an allotted amount of time to complete a set of activities. It can be incredibly helpful to implement the Pomodoro style of working as well. There are plenty of apps available to help you utilize this working style, but you can also use a simple kitchen timer like you've seen at

Grandma's.

The pomodoro technique frequently gets rave reviews as one of the best productivity methods. This technique was established by a developer in the 90's named Francesco Corilio. It's a simple system to implement. Alan Henry describes the system like this: "When faced with a large task or series of tasks, break the work down into short, timed intervals that are spaced out by short breaks. This trains your brain to focus for short periods and helps you stay on top of deadlines or constantly-refilling inboxes. With time it can even help improve your attention span and concentration."[1]

The process is even simpler than the description:

1. Choose a task.

2. Set your timer for 25 minutes (or a longer amount of time if you want more, two hours max for the highest levels of productivity and avoiding brain burnout).

3. Work diligently until the time is up.

4. Take a short break (up to 5 minutes)

By following this process, you can more easily focus, train your brain, and begin crossing things off your to-do list in a more efficient manner to quickly accomplish your goals. Utilizing the breaks in the sprints of work can help your brain feel recharged to push through the more intense work tasks you may have been putting off.

Analyze and maximize your work environment. The

---

[1] https://lifehacker.com/productivity-101-a-primer-to-the-pomodoro-technique-1598992730

environment in which you are working can greatly impact your productivity, which in turn will affect the results you obtain and the goals you reach. Make sure you're blocking out distractions like music with lyrics or responding to every ping immediately.

HOW TO REACH YOUR GOALS

1. Analyze and understand how you could utilize an effective and intentional goal.
2. Strategically outline your goals using the SMART format.
3. Have an accountability partner.
4. Maintain clarity about what achieving the goal will bring to your life.
5. Establish smaller action items to lead you to your goal.
6. Utilize your accountability partner for feedback.
7. Release yourself from judgement.
8. Write your goals down and place them in a place where you will see them regularly.
9. Stop multitasking.
10. Make sure your work environment is cultivating focus and productivity.

CHAPTER NINE

ORGANIZATION

As a top Sales Representative for Xerox Corporation, we were expected to have a completely clear desk before we left each night. Not a single sheet of paper should be left behind. The expectation was once you touched a piece of paper, you completed the task required then filed it.

Organization is important because it allows individuals and groups to perform tasks more efficiently. It helps people find information and items faster, and it allows groups to work together without wasting time. Organization is important for dealing with important information and client relations as well.

Imagine you have a vendor you're working closely with, an account manager who handles all your orders. One day you visit his office. When you go in and sit down, you notice there are papers all over his desk and his bookshelves are in disarray. What feeling does this imagery conjure up for you? Would you want to continue doing business with someone if they were that unorganized? How do you know this wouldn't cause an issue with your orders or the things you need from this vendor?

Organization is key to a clean mind and higher efficiency. It also reflects greatly on your work ethic to those looking in and can have a detrimental impact on important sales relationships when not implemented effectively.

WHY IS ORGANIZATION IMPORTANT?

Organization lays the foundation for morale, efficiency, and deeper thinking. According to David Levitin, a professor of psychology and behavioral neuroscience at McGill University, the conscious mind can only focus on up to four things at one time. Through better organization, you can better focus your mind and work more efficiently.

Researchers from Princeton University conducted a study around clutter in 2011. They found clutter can make it more difficult to focus on certain tasks. "They found that the visual cortex can be overwhelmed by task-irrelevant objects, making it harder to allocate attention and complete tasks efficiently."[2]

Being organized provides peace of mind for your clients. If a client sees a disorganized desk, they can become concerned their account and information will be handled in the same disorganized fashion. Disorganization can also cause bottlenecks in your work process. When a client sees an unorganized workspace, they can become concerned with your ability to process their work quickly enough for their liking.

Efficiency is key in the sales field. The number of sales you make and the commission you generate are both based on how efficiently you work. By maintaining an organized work process and clutter-free workspace, you will find the

---

[2] https://www.psychologytoday.com/us/blog/the-truisms-wellness/201607/the-powerful-psychology-behind-cleanliness

things you need to work quickly, generate sales more efficiently, and meet your goals and quota, resulting in better employee reviews and more money in your pocket.

I remember when I worked at Xerox and I was sent out on a day of sales calls with our top sales performer. His name was Ted S. I have never seen a sale representative who wasted less time. Ted's entire day was occupied with activities to get customers, follow up with prospective customers, perform administrative tasks or close sales. He had the most clear, precise, and well-organized system for sales I had ever seen. He almost seemed like a robot.

As a man who set clear goals in front of him, he then analyzed his system so he could be the most organized *to reach those goals.*

His schedule looked something like this:

7 am – arrive in the office and go through leads

8 am – leave office to do office visits

12 pm – break for lunch

12:15 pm – follow up on emails for new leads

1 pm – finish office visits

4 pm – finalize paperwork for the day in the office

6 pm – home for family time

Ted S. knew why he was working and what needed to be done to get where he needed to be.

Through effective organization, he was able to consistently be the top salesman for 15 years at Xerox. Clients knew they could rely on him because of his dependability and efficiency.

Why do we like and crave organization so much? Our desire for organization is rooted in our very design. Even at our atomic core, we are well-organized. Our bodies are made up of millions of integrated biological systems. These systems are highly organized, efficient, and operate on closely calculated schedules and rhythms. Without this organization, we would be in medical disarray.

WAYS TO BE ORGANIZED

It is vital organization is implemented throughout the different aspects of your life and work process. From communication to time management to the physical office you work in, organization can streamline your work and keep up appearances vital to all your sales relationships.

Technology can make getting organized a little easier, but it comes with drawbacks. There are plenty of apps, tools, and systems to assist you with getting organized. However, there is a time investment required to set up and fully understand these tools. Once the tools are implemented, they are generally much easier to maintain than a physical system in the office.

It can be highly beneficial to implement the use of a physical planner. As previously mentioned, your conscious brain can only focus on about 4 tasks at a time. This means if you are constantly thinking about the next things you need to do or the errands you need to run later then you aren't giving the tasks in front of you your full attention. By writing things down, it turns your big picture plan into bite-size action pieces for you to accomplish. This makes it easier for your brain to focus on the tasks in front of you instead of getting distracted by the bigger goals.[3]

Get creative. It can be hard to maintain an organization system but coming up with inspiring and engaging creative solutions makes it easier to stay motivated. Creative solutions include strategies such as creating visual reminders for things you need to do regularly. Do you have tasks that pop up on the same day each month? Create a generic calendar and mark those dates. Then place the calendar next to your computer so you will see it regularly for the reminder. Do you find you work better when you do long sprints of work and then take a mental break? Get a FitBit tracker, which will remind you to get moving each hour or on a schedule you set!

DO'S AND DON'TS OF ORGANIZATION

Don't try to do everything in one day. If you haven't had a clear organization system in place, trying to implement one in every aspect of your life in one day will be overwhelming.

Do make an implementation plan. Analyze how you work and what would best suit you. As Levitin stated in his interview with *The Washington Post*[4], some people are

---

[3] https://www.fastcompany.com/3063392/how-writing-to-do-lists-helps-your-brain-even-when-you-dont-comple

[4] https://www.washingtonpost.com/news/on-leadership/wp/2014/09/08/what-neuroscience-tells-us-about-getting-organized/?utm_term=.a2682874e934

pilers and some people are filers. Filing everything away will not work for every person. Take some time to do a little research about different organizational styles and tips to help you find what will work best for you.

Don't waste time organizing clutter. We tend to hold on to things longer than necessary in the off chance we need it in the future. For example, there are probably a few papers and files from old clients in your office you could shred to clear out the space. If you are concerned you may need this information in the future, scan it to have a digital copy on hand and shred the physical copy.

Do invest a little of your time in decluttering before you organize everything. Sort through your old client files. Dump files you no longer need and organize paperwork on potential leads and current clients.

Don't work sporadically. Just as we talked about in the chapter on goals, it's important to block out your schedule and focus on the task in front of you instead of trying to multi-task or bounce back and forth between tasks.

Do plan out your organization. There are many different tips, tricks, and styles you can use to get organized. Take some time to investigate various styles. Then, considering your current organizational style and habits, make adjustments and implement the style that best meets your needs.

Don't get discouraged. Getting organized can be a long process. Not only will you need time to understand and apply your new system of organization to your files and office, but you will also need time to adjust your working style. You've been working one way, unorganized, for a long time; it's imperative you take time to figure out how to incorporate this new system into your process. It's like when your company gets a new IT system, or you switch jobs--there's a bit of a learning curve and growing pains to overcome, but once you master it, it will revitalize your work life.

Do enlist someone from your company or a business mentor to help you along the way. This will keep you accountable and provide you with someone to turn to when you get discouraged or even frustrated.

HOW TO GET ORGANIZED

1. Start with removing as much of the physical clutter as you can.

2. Research organization tips and tricks to find a style that works for you.

3. Enlist an accountability partner for feedback and to stay on track.

4. Clear out your visual area so you can better focus on the tasks in front of you.

5. Convert old files into digital formats to cut down on physical clutter.

6. Get a planner and USE IT.

7. Start small and plan out your organization so you don't get overwhelmed.

8. Implement digital tools like a Pomodoro timer or Google Drive.

9. Get creative with your reminders.

CHAPTER TEN

DILIGENCE

*And God gave Solomon wisdom **and exceedingly great understanding, and largeness of heart like the sand on the seashore...For he was wiser than all men.** 1 Kings 4:29-31*

And all the kings of earth sought the **presence of Solomon to hear his wisdom,** *which God had put in his heart 2 Chronicles 9:23*

Diligence is a learned skill that combines strategic persistence and planning executed in a timely manner with a goal in mind to meet or exceed expectations; a continuous commitment to doing the job correct the first time.

Wisdom and Understanding: Wisdom is knowing the truth and how to apply it to any given situation. Understanding is knowledge seasoned and modified by wisdom and insight. Solomon exhorts, "Wisdom is the principle thing. Therefore, get wisdom, and in all your getting, get understanding."

WHO WAS KING SOLOMON?

Training and occupation: As a member of the royal court, Solomon would have had access to the best education possible, likely including all types of tutors. He would have been trained in the ways of the court, warfare and how to run a nation. Solomon's occupation was being a king. Solomon's reign was Israel's most prosperous and powerful period. From a worldly standpoint, he was the most successful king in Israel's history.

Place in history: Solomon was the third king of Israel. He was the king of Israel during its golden age. He built the temple during his rule, known as one of the seven wonders of the ancient world. He was responsible for many cultural and architectural achievements. Solomon penned much of Proverbs and Ecclesiastes and was the subject of Song of Solomon.

Special traits: Solomon possessed extreme wisdom. 1 Kings 3:10-28, 1 Kings 4:30-34, 5:12, 10:1-10, 10:22-25. The story following God's answer to Solomon's prayer for wisdom is written to illustrate Solomon's wisdom in action. There would be many such cases of disagreements between the citizens of his country requiring wisdom to reach a resolution. Keep in mind there wasn't DNA evidence, closed caption video, fingerprinting, or other elaborate methods for determining the truth in Solomon's time. A lot of times it boiled down to one person's word against another's.

Solomon's strengths were not on the battlefield but in the realm of the mind--an understanding heart to judge, mediation, planning, working with excellence, and organization. Solomon's writings demonstrate to us how to order our values, which lead to character. Character leads to wholeness, and wholeness leads to satisfaction. They are designed to warn us of pitfalls along the way.

KING SOLOMON'S PRAYER TO GOD

Then Solomon said, "You have shown great lovingkindness to your servant David my father, according as he walked before you in truth and righteousness and uprightness of heart toward you; and you have reserved for him this great lovingkindness, that you have given him a son to sit on his throne, as it is this day. "Now, O LORD my God, You have made Your servant king in place of my father David, yet I am but a little child; I do not know how to go out or come in. "Your servant is in the midst of your people which you have chosen, a great people who are too many to be numbered or counted. "So give your servant an understanding heart to judge your people to discern between good and evil. For who is able to judge this great people of yours?" 1 Kings 3:6-9

GOD'S ANSWER

It was pleasing in the sight of the Lord that Solomon had asked this thing. God said to him, "Because you have asked this thing and have not asked for yourself long life, nor have asked riches for yourself, nor have you asked for the life of your enemies, but have asked for yourself discernment to understand justice, behold, I have done according to your words. Behold, I have given you a wise and discerning heart, so that there has been no one like you before you, nor shall one like you arise after you. "I have also given you what you have not asked, both riches and honor, so that there will not be any among the kings like you all your days. "If you walk in my ways, keeping my statutes and commandments, as your father David walked, then I will prolong your days."

Then Solomon awoke, and behold, it was a dream. And he came to Jerusalem and stood before the ark of the covenant of the Lord, and offered burnt offerings and made peace offerings, and made a feast for all his servants. 1 Kings 3:10-15

EXAMPLE OF KINGS SOLOMON WISDOM JUDGES DILIGENTLY

Then two women who were harlots came to the king and stood before him. The one woman said, "Oh, my lord, this woman and I live in the same house; and I gave birth to a child while she was in the house. "It happened on the third day after I gave birth, that this woman also gave birth to a child, and we were together. There was no stranger with us in the house, only the two of us in the house. "This woman's son died in the night, because she lay on it. "So she arose in the middle of the night and took my son from beside me while your maidservant slept, and laid him in her bosom, and laid her dead son in my bosom. "When I rose in the morning to nurse my son, behold, he was dead; but when I looked at him carefully in the morning, behold, he was not my son, whom I had borne." Then the other woman said, "No! For the living one is my son, and the dead one is your son." But the first woman said, "No! For the dead one is your son, and the living one is my son." Thus they spoke before the king.

Then the king said, "The one says, 'This is my son who is living, and your son is the dead one'; and the other says, 'No! For your son is the dead one, and my son is the living one.'" The king said, "Get me a sword." So they brought a sword before the king. The king said, "Divide the living child in two, and give half to the one and half to the other." Then the woman whose child was the living one spoke to the king, for she was deeply stirred over her son and said, "Oh, my lord, give her the living child, and by no means kill him." But the other said, "He shall be neither mine nor yours; divide him!" Then the king said, "Give the first woman the living child, and by no means kill him. She is his mother." When all Israel heard of the judgment which the king had handed down, they feared the king, for they saw that the wisdom of God was in him to administer justice. 1 Kings 3:16-28

Throughout the story of Solomon's life, interjections about his great wisdom are made. This is clearly an important aspect of Solomon's leadership. Prioritize wisdom. Seek after and cherish understanding. Realize knowledge without wisdom and understanding can be futile. Apply your heart to wisdom, pay attention and turn your ear to wisdom and understanding. You must embrace them both. You will be able to rest assured that patience, discernment, favor, prosperity, safety, and favor with others will be the result.

9 DILIGENCE KEYS SOLOMON RECOMMENDS

1. **Consider the ant and her characteristics** (Proverbs chapter 6:6-8)

> [6] *Go to the ant, thou sluggard; consider her ways, and be wise:*
> [7] *Which having no guide, overseer, or ruler,*
> [8] *Provideth her meat in the summer, and gathers her food in the harvest.*

Do you know any sluggards/lazy Sales Representatives? This is a term rarely used in our world today. The first thing I think of when hearing this word are creeping, slimy slugs.

You could easily identify what a sluggard is if I gave you some synonyms. How do these words grab you – lazy, sluggish, loafer, slacker, and couch potato? Are you getting the picture now?

Solomon has a lot to say about the lazy. This passage in Proverbs 6 may be the best known of them all, mostly because it tells us to consider the ant – an animal we hardly ever pay attention to.

I don't consider the ant much. The only time I really notice them is when one is crawling on me or I see a big mound of Florida ants build sand piles nine inches tall on the corners of the sidewalks. Here's a public service announcement – if you see one of those don't step in it. The ants will swarm you for sure.

Yet here in Proverbs 6:6, they are presented as a model of work ethic. In fact, the sluggard is encouraged to *"Go to the ant"* and *"Consider her ways..."* In other words, sluggard salesperson, Solomon is shouting at you "Pay attention to what the ant does...you could learn a thing or two about working diligently".

In the next few verses, Solomon goes on to describe some interesting things related to the work ethic of the ant. Here is the description in its entirety:

> *Go to the ant, you sluggard!*
> *Consider her ways and be wise.*
> *Which, having no captain, overseer or ruler,*
> *Provides her supplies in the summer,*
> *And gathers her food in the harvest. Proverbs 6:6-8*

So much can be drawn out of these verses, but there are three big conclusions you should be aware of related to work ethic:

1. **The ant motivates itself.** We see here the ant has no captain. There is no overseer or ruler telling the ant what to do. The ant knows what to do and motivates itself to accomplish the task.

2. **The ant looks out for itself.** The ant provides for her own needs. She gathers her supplies (literally *bread* or *meat*) when needed. She is not looking to someone else to provide for her. It's up to her and she knows it.

3. **The ant pushes itself.** There is a season for everything, and during the harvest the ant gathers her food. When it's time–when the really hard work needs to be done–she doesn't shy away from it. She pushes herself to gather what's needed when the time is right. The reward for her industrious work is a bountiful supply of food that will sustain her going forward.

2. **Proverbs 10:4 He becometh poor that dealeth with a slack hand: but Proverbs the hand of the diligent maketh rich.**

He becomes poor that deals [with] a slack hand...

A slack hand is either remiss in giving to the necessities of others, according to his abilities, and as cases require; or negligent and slothful in business. This is one "that worketh with a deceitful hand"; or, "with a hand of deceit" [1], as it may be rendered; who pretends to work, but does not; who makes a show as if he did, but acts deceitfully; or who uses many tricking and deceitful ways and methods to live, as slothful persons usually do.

...but the hand of the diligent maketh rich; that is, with the blessing of God along with it, as in (Proverbs 10:22); such who are "sharp" and acute, as the word signifies; who are careful and industrious, mind their business, and do the honest part; these, with a divine blessing, frequently grow rich: or rather who are like those that dig in the earth for gold, who search for it with great eagerness and diligence.

3. **Proverb 11:27 He that diligently seeketh good procureth favour: but he that seeketh mischief, it shall come unto him.**

Observe, 1. Those who are industrious to do good in the world get themselves beloved both with God and man: *He that rises early to that which is good*, who seeks opportunities to serve friends and relieve the poor, and lays out himself therein, *procures favor*. All around him love him, speak well of him, and will be ready to do him a kindness; and, better than that, better than life, he has God's lovingkindness. 2. Those who are industrious to do mischief are preparing ruin for themselves: *It shall come unto them;* some time or other they will be paid in their own coin. And, observe, *seeking mischief* is here set in opposition to *seeking good;* for those who are not doing good are doing mischief.

4. **Proverbs 12:1: "He who loves instruction loves knowledge, but he who hates correction is unwise."** If you believe you are correct all the time, this is for you. Pride can get in the way of taking instructions or good counsel. We all make mistakes. Don't be threatened. Open up to accept and encourage constructive criticism, especially from

your employees who understand the business. Some of the best ideas can come from customers and employees.

I worked as a general sales manager for Saturn, where our employee and customer satisfaction surveys raised the bar for customer feedback for all car dealerships. The customers had to rate their experience for satisfaction in a number of critical areas. These areas were benchmarked by the standards set at the corporate office. If your customer satisfaction surveys dipped below a 90 percent A grade in any of the 10 areas evaluated, the dealership was penalized monthly and had to create an action plan to bring the standards up to par. Often customers would have suggestions for how we could improve the customers' experience. We would take these suggestions to corporate and corporate would evaluate them. If they agreed with a suggestion, it would become part of the new process. By creating an environment that encourages suggestions and criticism, you can greatly improve your process or sales and allow employees and customers to feel like a valued part of the business.

5. Proverbs 12:24 **The hand of the diligent will rule, But the slack hand will be put to forced labor.** The hand of the diligent shall bear rule — Industry is the way to promotion. An instance of this is found in 1 Kings 11:28, where we learn Solomon advanced Jeroboam because he saw he was an

industrious young man. Men who take pleasure in enduring and perfecting the challenges in honest employment, and especially those who labor to be useful to others, will thereby gain such an interest and reputation. The person who has been faithful in a few things will be made ruler over many things. Those who are diligent while they are young frequently procure the steadfastness, wisdom, and stick-to-it-ness to gain leadership, understanding, wealth and power, which enable them to rule.

6. **Proverbs 14:23 in all labor there is profit, but mere talk leads only to poverty.**

Simply put, Solomon warns us that which is cheap and easy leads to poverty. Diligence in working should be demanding. If we are not displaying success in our career, then we are probably not being diligent enough.

7. **Proverbs 22:29 Do you see a man diligent in his business? He shall stand before Kings.**

I started a Safe Teen Driving Non-Profit organization in Orange County Florida in 2014. Teen crashes had risen 86 percent in one year. I partnered with the Florida Highway Patrol, Florida Department of Transportation, Orlando Health Trauma Center and 26,000 Students at 21 High Schools. The first two years, we worked mostly as volunteers with high school PTA meetings and student sporting events, staying diligent to the task of raising awareness and getting the crash prevention message out to students to reduce crashes in Orange County. It was a noble effort. However, none of the agencies we partnered with were willing to give us funding to support our efforts. We couldn't even get brochures from FDOT to reference Safe Teen Driving due to budget cutbacks. This was very disheartening. I was getting discouraged. Just as I was pondering quitting, I spoke to one of the board members, Archie Denard, who had been working in Student Transportation and Safety for over 30 Years. He said "Virgil, if you stay diligent to this work, you will meet the right partner who will solve your money challenges." Two weeks later, the Florida Virtual Schools Driver Education Department (over 12,000 a semester registered) called me. They had heard about the work our organization was doing in the community. They invited me to speak at their first Safe Teen Driving Outing. Something about Archie's words of encouragement rang true in my heart. I decided I would go and speak at the event. While at the event, one of the department heads heard my speech and requested we write a proposal for their organization. As a result of that meeting, Florida Virtual Schools' Drivers Education Department is now partnering with our safe teen driving initiative with a $257,000.00 annual grant. Diligence paid off and placed me in the presence of very influential decision makers.

8. **Proverbs 21:5 The plans of the diligent lead surely to advantage.** Solomon assures us the plans of those who are diligent will lead to their advantage. It doesn't matter if you're competing with other sales professionals; you will have a distinct advantage.

9. **Proverbs 24:6 By wise counsel thou shalt make thy war; and in the multitude of counselors there is safety.** Solomon is specifically talking about war in this case, but his recommendation also applies to the field of selling. Seek wise counsel before you initiate actions. This will allow you to make careful and deliberate choices and choose your battles wisely.

FOUR DAILY STEPS TO BECOME MORE DILIGENT AT WORK

1. **Remove distractions.** Too much time on the internet, your phone or in front of the television can distract you from your goals. It is easy to get off task if your phone is going off or you have social media tabs open on your computer while you're working.

- There are apps to help you remove distractions for certain periods of time.
- You can turn off notifications on your phone or turn on the "do not disturb" setting.

2. **Keep yourself organized with to-do lists.** You can make separate lists for urgent, high-priority, and low-priority tasks, or you can make lists by date. For example, you can list all the tasks you need to do today on one list, and all the things you need to complete tomorrow on another. By knowing what you want to accomplish, you can get more done. Breaking larger tasks into smaller steps can help you see the overall time a task will take and its potential complexity. You can schedule time for each task or subtask. Keeping the list to three items can help you focus and get things done

3. **Prioritize.** Pushing back other things of less importance can help you focus on tasks that will help you reach your goals. Deadlines can help you determine what's important, as well as considering the impact completing or not completing a task will have on you and your employer.

   For instance, you can wait to answer a non-urgent email from a friend you see regularly when you're working on a work project. If you're uncertain what to prioritize, ask your manager.

4. **Use time efficiently.** Making a schedule and having a plan for the day will help you see how you are using your time. This is where you can set deadlines, make appointments, and schedule breaks. Remember to give yourself enough time for each task.

ABOUT THE AUTHOR

Virgil Blocker is a sales professional and business owner with over twenty years of sales experience. During his tenure at Xerox Corp, Virgil was a top five percent sales performer and became the number one regional salesman for the company. He is also a fifteen-time President's Club award recipient, achieving this distinction for multiple years at both Eastman Kodak and Danka Office Imaging. He has received the Billy T. Fowles' Outstanding Training Award and was voted Outstanding Sales Manager for General Motors. Virgil has drawn on his extensive experience as a top sales performer and sales coach to author his first book, 10 Principles in the Life or Death of a Salesperson. Virgil speaks to and coaches sales professionals seeking to be consistent high performers using the principles espoused in his book. He currently lives and works in Central Florida.

www.ingramcontent.com/pod-product-compliance
Lightning Source LLC
Chambersburg PA
CBHW052017230326
41598CB00078B/3527

9 781732 713208